Easy-To-Make Mocktail Recipes

Non Alcoholic Drinks To Serve At Your Parties!

BY

MOLLY MILLS

Copyright © 2021 by Molly Mills

License Notes

No part of this book may be copied, replicated, distributed, sold or shared without the express and written consent of the Author.

The ideas expressed in the book are for entertainment purposes. The Reader assumes all risk when following any guidelines and the Author accepts no responsibility if damages occur due to actions taken by the Reader.

Table of Contents

Introduction 6

    Watermelon Margarita 8

    Raspberry Sparkle 10

    Pineapple-Orange Punch 12

    Cranberry-Basil Sangria 14

    Lemon-Basil Mojito Mocktail 16

    Ginger-Lime Beer Mocktail 18

    Negroni Mocktail 20

    Lime-Mint Sparklers 22

    Apple Cider Mule 24

    Strawberry-Chamomile Martini 26

    Purple Lemonade 28

    Piña Colada Mocktail 30

    Virgin Hurricanes 32

    Popsicle Punch 34

Frozen Margarita Mocktail.. 36

Mulled Wine Mocktail 38

Watermelon Bellini Mocktail 40

Fizzy Cranberry Punch 42

Sensational Slushie 44

Classic Shirley Temple 46

White Russian Mocktail 48

Grapefruit Agua Fresca 50

Whiskey Sour Mocktail 52

Strawberry Daiquiri Mocktail 54

Cucumber-Lemonade Mocktail 56

Banana Punch 58

Orange Julius Mocktail 60

Peach Bellini Mocktail 62

Booze-Free French 75 64

Butterbeer 66

Conclusion 68

About the Author 69

Don't Miss Out! 70

Introduction

If you are not really a fan of alcohol or you simply cannot have it, you don't have to settle for boring beverages, you know! There are tasty mixes that you can make anytime you need to. That's where mocktails come in. They are the perfect substitutes for booze-driven drinks, so you get the flavors minus the spirits. That way, you will not have to wonder what a sangria or a margarita taste like. These mocktails taste the same but the alcohol content is omitted. Intrigued? Well, you don't have to be because we have a list of delicious mocktail recipes that you can use every day.

We can't blame you, the mocktail recipes in this cookbook sound so interesting. Go ahead and start picking your choice at the moment and make it. The ingredients are mostly just right at the pantry!

Watermelon Margarita

Are you looking for a margarita that is very fruity and absolutely tequila-free? Well, here it is. It is a watermelon concoction and it is so refreshing and tasty you wouldn't be able to get enough of it! A margarita cocktail is a favorite pick, especially for the ladies because of its artsy character. But by doing this mocktail, you will be able to impress even the kids with a delightful drink!

Serving size: 4

Prep Time: 5 mins

Ingredients:

- 1 pc seedless watermelon, cut into chunks
- 5 tbsp sparking water
- 4 tsp agave syrup
- ½ cup fresh lime juice

Instructions:

1. Puree watermelon chunks in a blender, add in lime juice and agave syrup and pulse again until combined.

2. Pour into 4 individual glasses, spoon over sparkling water, and serve.

Raspberry Sparkle

Here is a sparkling and refreshing concoction that's perfect for all occasions. It requires only 4 ingredients and will only take you a few minutes to make a good batch. This is a nice beverage you can prepare when your child's friends come over for an afternoon snack. Serve this with their favorite cookies and chips and they will have the time of their lives chilling the day away.

Serving size: 4

Prep Time: 3 mins

Ingredients:

- 8oz raspberry syrup
- 4 cups club soda, chilled
- 4oz red grapefruit juice
- 2 cups crushed ice

Instructions:

1. Stir together the ingredients in a large pitcher until well blended.

2. Serve and enjoy.

Pineapple-Orange Punch

Here is a sherbet punch that has a lot of punch! Don't get us wrong because the kick of this drink is very nice – it will not make you tipsy or dizzy or anything. It's like a beverage dessert with its tropical flavors that are refreshing and very nice to the palate at the same time. What's more, this recipe can serve a crowd and within only 10 minutes!

Serving size: 24

Prep Time: 10 mins

Ingredients:

- 7 cups fruit punch, chilled
- 1 (48oz) carton orange sherbet, softened
- 1 (46oz) can pineapple juice
- 1 pc orange, sliced into rounds
- ½ cup pineapple chunks
- 1 L ginger ale

Instructions:

1. Mix the orange sherbet and pineapple juice in a punch bowl until well blended.

2. Pour in fruit punch and ginger ale.

3. Serve with orange slices and pineapple chunks as a garnish.

Cranberry-Basil Sangria

A bottle of sangria always makes a party bright. But what if you want to serve it without the alcohol? Here comes this incredibly bright sangria mocktail that you can make with whatever fruits might be in season. For this particular recipe, however, we are going for the cranberry and basil mix.

Serving size: 4

Prep Time: 10 mins

Ingredients:

- 1/3 cup frozen cranberries
- ¼ cup basil leaves
- 1 pc orange, sliced
- 1 pc apple, cored and sliced
- 3 cups cranberry juice
- ½ cup fresh orange juice
- 1 (12oz) can seltzer
- 2 cups ice cubes

Instructions:

1. Mix together cranberry and orange juices, plus seltzer in a pitcher.

2. Stir in basil and orange and apple slices.

3. Pour into glasses over ice cubes and serve.

Lemon-Basil Mojito Mocktail

A classic mojito has rum, lime, and mint. In this mocktail version, however, we dropped the rum and then exchanged lime and mint for lemon and basil. Did they make a difference? Well, taste it to prove it! This drink mix is so easy to make and so fun to be creative with as well. If you like the boozed version, you simply need to bring back the rum!

Serving size: 12

Prep Time: 15 mins

Ingredients:

- 1 pc lemon, sliced into wedges
- 1 ½ cups sugar
- 6 cups fresh basil leaves, divided
- 2 (1L) bottles club soda
- 4 cups water
- 5 cups crushed ice, divided

Instructions:

1. Whisk together sugar and water in a small saucepan and heat on medium fire until the sugar is properly dissolved.

2. Add in 3 cups of the basil leaves and turn off the heat.

3. Using the back of the spoon or a pestle, crush the basil leaves until the aromatic flavors are released. Set aside to cool down completely.

4. When the basil mixture is ready, transfer to a large pitcher with crushed ice and club soda.

5. Stir in the remaining basil leaves, plus lemon wedges, and serve.

Ginger-Lime Beer Mocktail

Here is a beer that is not really beer. It's a fizzy summer drink with only a few ingredients, including the delightfully refreshing ginger and lime. Those two key ingredients make this drink not just alcohol-free but also somewhat healthy. It's a great option for a party with kids and teens. They will love the taste.

Serving size: 8

Prep Time: 10 mins

Ingredients:

- ½ cup ginger beer, chilled
- 1 pc lime, sliced into rounds
- 1 ½ tbsp fresh lime juice
- ¼ cup orange juice, chilled
- 2 tbsp maple syrup
- 3 tbsp simple syrup, chilled
- ¼ tsp orange bitters
- 2 cups ice cubes

Instructions:

1. Stir all the ingredients in a large pitcher, except for the lime wheels.

2. Serve in glasses with a garnish of a lime wheel and some ice cubes.

Negroni Mocktail

Negroni is a popular cocktail made with gin, a fortified red wine, and an Italian liqueur. But with all those booze ingredients taken out, we are bringing in grape juice and special syrup. It may not taste as close to the classic but it is definitely a welcome substitute, especially when you only want something nice to enjoy a chillout night.

Serving size: 1

Prep Time: 20 mins

Ingredients:

- ½ pc grapefruit, sliced into chunks
- ½ pc orange, sliced
- 3 pcs cardamom pods, lightly crushed
- Pinch of coriander seeds
- ¼ cup caster sugar
- 2 drops red food coloring
- ¼ cup white grape juice
- ¼ cup water
- ½ cup ice

Instructions:

1. Place grapefruit chunks, orange slices, cardamom, coriander, and sugar in a saucepan and heat on medium for about 5 minutes, stirring occasionally and crushing the solids using the back of the spoon.

2. Turn off the heat and stir in the red food coloring. Stir to combine, then set aside to cool completely.

3. Strain the grapefruit mixture and discard the solids.

4. Prepare a tall glass with ice, pour in the prepared syrup, plus grape juice and water.

5. Stir and serve.

Lime-Mint Sparklers

Lime and mint make a nice pair, especially if you make them into a beverage. They are huge on flavors but are very light on the budget. For this fizzy drink, for example, you only need to add some soda water and lime cordial and you have a drink!

Serving size: 8

Prep Time: 10 mins

Ingredients:

- 8 pcs limes, quartered
- 2/3 cup fresh mint leaves, finely chopped
- ½ cup lime cordial
- 1 ¼ L soda water, chilled
- 2 cups ice cubes

Instructions:

1. Combine lime and mint in a pitcher and gently crush with the back of a spoon.

2. Stir in lime cordial and ice cubes until well blended.

3. Pour in soda water and serve.

Apple Cider Mule

A classic mule that's loaded with vodka is definitely something that could easily brighten up any party. But serving a mule minus the vodka would not easily taste any different, if ever, it could even be a more delicious substitute. That is, if you are making this Apple Cider Mule recipe. Let's go and start with the recipe!

Serving size: 1

Prep Time: 5 mins

Ingredients:

- 4oz ginger beer, chilled
- 2oz apple cider, chilled
- 1 tsp apple cider vinegar
- 1 tsp maple syrup
- ½ cup ice cubes

Instructions:

1. Mix together apple cider, vinegar, and maple syrup in a mule cup until well blended.

2. Add ice and pour over ginger beer.

3. Serve and enjoy.

Strawberry-Chamomile Martini

A martini cocktail is such a classy drink. It's a nice addition to make parties wonderful. It's basically made with gin and aromatic wine and it tastes really delicious. Don't fret because dropping the alcohol content will not make it any different. It's wonderful and tasty. You will continue to impress your guests with this drink, especially because it is alcohol-free.

Serving size: 1

Prep Time: 5 mins

Ingredients:

- 1 pc strawberry
- ½ pc orange, sliced into wedges
- 1 pc lemon, sliced into wedges
- 5 pcs mint leaves
- 1oz elderflower cordial
- 4oz chamomile
- 2 tbsp ginger juice
- 2 tbsp simple syrup
- ½ cup crushed ice

Instructions:

1. Stir together strawberry, orange, lemon, ginger juice, and simple syrup. Gently crush the strawberry using the back of the spoon.

2. Add elderflower cordial, chamomile, and mint leaves, plus ice.

3. Strain liquid into your martini glass and serve.

Purple Lemonade

What's a better beverage than a refreshing lemonade? Yes! A purple lemonade! Although there is not much of a difference in taste, presentation is a huge factor. That makes this a wonderful addition to this mocktail recipe book. Just like the other drink mixes, you can serve this anytime, from parties to picnics to every snack time. And it has no alcohol content!

Serving size: 4

Prep Time: 5 mins

Ingredients:

- 2 cups lemon juice
- 1 pc lemon, slice into rounds
- 3 tbsp dried lavender
- ¼ cup honey
- ½ cup sugar
- 6 cups water, divided
- Few drops of purple food coloring
- 2 cups ice cubes

Instructions:

1. Stir together sugar and about 2 cups of water in a small saucepan and heat on medium-low until sugar is dissolved.

2. Turn off the fire and add in lavender, plus honey. Stir to combine, then set aside to cool down.

3. Strain the syrup, discarding the solids and transfer to a pitcher.

4. Add the remaining ingredients and stir.

5. Serve and enjoy.

Piña Colada Mocktail

There is nothing more delightful than a guilt-free piña colada that has no alcohol but has all the flavors. This drink is so festive and nice. If you really want to make an impression, go ahead and do the extra mile of decorating your serving glasses, it could just be a few pineapple slices or a cocktail umbrella!

Serving size: 1

Prep Time: 15 mins

Ingredients:

- ½ cup pineapple juice
- 2 tbsp lime juice
- ¼ cup coconut milk
- 1 pc cherry
- 1 pc cinnamon stick
- 5 pcs cloves
- 5 pcs black peppercorns
- 1 cup muscovado sugar
- ½ cup ice cubes
- 2 cups water

Instructions:

1. Stir together muscovado sugar and water in a saucepan and heat on medium low.

2. Let it simmer gently while stirring constantly until the sugar is dissolved.

3. Add cinnamon stick, cloves, and peppercorns, then, let it boil before turning off the heat. Set aside to cool completely.

4. Once the syrup is cool enough, strain the syrup into a jar, discarding the solids. This may keep for up to three days in the fridge.

5. Meanwhile, stir together pineapple juice, lime juice, coconut milk, and ice in a jug.

6. Stir and pour into a glass, pour about 2 tablespoons of prepared syrup, and garnish with a piece of cherry before serving.

Virgin Hurricanes

The original hurricane is in no way subtle. But since we are doing mocktails, this one has such a significant kick but it is meant to impress guests all the same. It's a nice refresher with all its fruity goodness with as much sparkle to make fizz.

Serving size: 8

Prep Time: 10 mins

Ingredients:

- 1 cup unsweetened pineapple juice
- 2 cups passion fruit juice
- 1 cup orange juice
- ¾ cup lemon juice
- 8pcs pineapple wedges
- 8 pcs maraschino cherries
- 2 cups carbonated water
- 2 cups ice cubes

Instructions:

1. Stir pineapple, passion fruit, orange, and lemon juices in a large pitcher.

2. Pour in carbonated water and gently stir, then pour onto individual glasses with ice.

3. Garnish each with a piece of pineapple wedge and a cherry on top.

4. Serve and enjoy.

Popsicle Punch

What's a better way to enjoy a delicious punch at an outdoor barbecue party? Serve them with popsicle sticks as flavored coolers. You simply have to pull out a fruity popsicle recipe that will blend well with your drink mix and you will surely keep everyone impressed!

Serving size: 6

Prep Time: 10 mins

Ingredients:

- 3 pcs mango fruit pops
- 3 pcs strawberry fruit pops
- 2 pcs mangoes, cubed
- 1 cup strawberries, sliced
- 4 cups lemon lime soda
- 4 cups lemonade
- 1 (12oz) can seltzer

Instructions:

1. Stir all the ingredients in a large pitcher, except for the fruit pops until well blended.

2. To serve, place individual glasses with a fruit pop, pour in the mocktail mix, and garnish with more strawberry and mango slices.

Frozen Margarita Mocktail

We know that it's hard to get over a margarita mocktail. So, we came up with another! This time, it's a frozen booze-free drink that's festive enough to be present at your summer parties and special dinners. They work perfectly with good food, good company, and a nice and chill ambiance. Now, that's what a holiday is like!

Serving size: 4

Prep Time: 10 mins

Ingredients:

- ¾ cup orange juice
- 2/3 cup unsweetened grapefruit juice
- 1 (6oz) can frozen limeade concentrate
- 1 pc lime, sliced into wedges
- 4 tbsp coarse sugar
- 4 cups ice cubes

Instructions:

1. Stir together orange and grapefruit juice, plus frozen limeade and ice in a blender and pulse until smooth and slushy.

2. Place sugar on a plate, rub lime wedges on the rim of your serving glasses and dip them onto sugar.

3. Pour in a frozen margarita and serve.

Mulled Wine Mocktail

A homemade hot wine seems like a good idea, unless you are about to serve a crowd with non-alcohol drinkers. That makes this mocktail useful. It's a fruity beverage recipe with some kick. It's as warming as the real deal but without the booze, of course.

Serving size: 6

Prep Time: 10 mins

Ingredients:

- 5 cups pomegranate juice
- 2 cups apple juice
- 1 pc orange, quartered
- 1 cup frozen blackberries
- 4 pcs cloves
- 1 pc star anise
- 1 pc cinnamon stick
- 3 pcs black peppercorns
- ¼ cup caster sugar

Instructions:

1. Combine sugar, pomegranate juice and apple juice, plus blackberries in a saucepan. Heat on medium-low fire, stirring gently to dissolve the sugar.

2. Add orange, cloves, star anise, cinnamon stick, and peppercorns. Let it simmer for a few minutes, then turn off the fire.

3. Transfer to heatproof glasses, discarding the solids.

4. Serve hot and enjoy.

Watermelon Bellini Mocktail

Simply put, a bellini is an Italian cocktail usually made with peaches and wine. Since we are supposed to come up with an alcohol-free drink, we dropped the wine. But that's not the only thing we did. We also switched watermelon for peaches for a more refreshing, totally fun beverage!

Serving size: 4

Prep Time: 5 mins

Ingredients:

- 1 cup watermelon, cubed
- 12oz sparkling cider

Instructions:

1. Place watermelon cubes in a blender or food processor and pulse until pureed.

2. Divide the watermelon puree equally into four individual glasses.

3. Pour in sparkling cider and garnish with more watermelon to garnish.

Fizzy Cranberry Punch

Here is another fruity, family-friendly drink that you can make in a good batch within just 5 minutes. Isn't that amazing? This is a great holiday drink, a wonderful summer beverage. It will blend well with any kind of food and will keep everyone entertained long before they have a nice sip. Oh, that wonderfully bright color of pink is so cool to the eyes.

Serving size: 12

Prep Time: 5 mins

Ingredients:

- 2 qt cranberry juice cocktail
- 1 (6oz) can pink lemonade concentrate
- 1 qt sparkling water

Instructions:

1. Stir all the ingredients in a large punch bowl or pitcher.

2. Serve and enjoy.

Sensational Slushie

Speaking of bright and colorful, here is another mocktail recipe you couldn't miss. It's loaded with a fresh fruity taste combined with some sparkle. Dress it up with a nice garnish like some fresh fruit slices and a playful straw and you are out to make a statement on your next party with such an incredible beverage offer!

Serving size: 20

Prep Time: 25 mins

Ingredients:

- 2 cups fresh strawberries, sliced
- 1 cup unsweetened pineapple juice
- 2 L lemon-lime soda, chilled
- 1 (12oz) can frozen lemonade concentrate, thawed
- 1 (12oz) can frozen limeade concentrate, thawed
- ½ cup sugar
- 3oz strawberry gelatin
- 2 cups boiling water
- 2 cups cold water

Instructions:

1. Dissolve sugar and gelatin in boiling water. Let it set.

2. Meanwhile, place strawberry slices and pineapple juice in a blender and pulse until combined.

3. In a large punch bowl, mix gelatin mixture and blended strawberries and pineapple juice.

4. Pour in soda and lemonade and limeade concentrates, plus water. Stir to blend.

5. Cover the bowl with a sheet of plastic wrap and freeze for about 8 hours or overnight.

6. Remove from the freezer about an hour before you are ready to serve.

Classic Shirley Temple

Unlike most of the drinks in this recipe book, a Shirley Temple has always been non-alcoholic. It's a classic drink made with grenadine, soda, and cherries. It's a delectably bubbly mix with some fruity flavors that both kids and adults alike would surely love.

Serving size: 4

Prep Time: 5 mins

Ingredients:

- 1 cup Maraschino cherries
- 4 tsp grenadine
- 3 cups lemon-lime soda
- Juice of 1 lime
- 2 cups ice

Instructions:

1. Divide ice cubes into four serving glasses.

2. Pour in soda and lime juice, then grenadine.

3. Serve with cherries as garnish.

White Russian Mocktail

The fantastic thing about mocktails is that you can enjoy all the flavors of the drink without having to worry about alcohol. So, you can serve them to everyone, across all ages. How do you do that in an elaborate cocktail recipe such as White Russian that requires vodka, making sure you are able to keep its bold flavors? Check out this recipe and you will soon find out how.

Serving size: 2

Prep Time: 5 mins

Ingredients:

- 4 tbsp salted caramel sauce, divided
- 2 tsp espresso powder
- ½ tsp unsweetened baking cocoa
- 6 tbsp heavy cream
- ½ cup water
- ½ cup ice cubes

Instructions:

1. Stir together 2 tablespoons of salted caramel sauce, espresso powder, cocoa, and water in a bowl.

2. Prepare two serving glasses, dipping the rim to the remaining caramel sauce.

3. Divide the caramel mixture between the glasses, add some ice, then cover the top with half of the cream each.

Grapefruit Agua Fresca

Agua Fresca has always been a wholesome drink. It's a Mexican mocktail that is simply made with water and fruit. But it is really more than just regular fruit juice. Like for this recipe, this grapefruit-laden drink mix, there's a lot of health benefits tucked in between with a subtle herbal flavor, thanks to the addition of kombucha, a fermented tea of sorts.

Serving size: 2

Prep Time: 2 mins

Ingredients:

- 1 cup grapefruit juice
- 1 cup unflavored kombucha
- 1 tsp maple syrup
- 2 pcs fresh rosemary sprigs
- 4 tbsp pure sparkling water

Instructions:

1. Stir together grapefruit juice, kombucha, plus maple syrup until well combined.

2. Divide into two serving glasses, top with 2 tablespoons of sparkling water each, and add a garnish of fresh rosemary sprigs.

Whiskey Sour Mocktail

Of course, the moment you hear whiskey, you can start thinking about getting tipsy. But you will never get close to being tipsy if you are served with this wonderful mocktail recipe that's loaded with lemon and some non-alcoholic malt. It's bubbly and refreshing and quite unique and interesting!

Serving size: 2

Prep Time: 5 mins

Ingredients:

- ½ cup fresh lemon juice
- 1 cup non-alcoholic spirit
- 4 tbsp simple syrup
- 1 pc egg white
- ½ tsp lemon zest

Instructions:

1. Place all the ingredients in a cocktail shaker, except for lemon zest, and shake vigorously until well combined.

2. Strain liquid into serving glasses, garnish with lemon zest, and serve.

Strawberry Daiquiri Mocktail

A daiquiri is another classic cocktail that's getting a no-booze makeover. We simply dropped the rum in the recipe and used strawberries and lemonade for a refreshing beverage everyone will surely love. If you want to go for the boozed kind, you simply put back the rum and that's it!

Serving size: 1

Prep Time: 5 mins

Ingredients:

- 2 pcs strawberries, hulled
- ¾ cup lemonade
- ¼ cup crushed ice

Instructions:

1. Place all the ingredients in a blender and pulse until smooth.

2. Pour into a glass and serve with a garnish of freshly sliced strawberries.

Cucumber-Lemonade Mocktail

This lemonade is more than just a drink. It's a piece of art. With a thin film of cucumber pressed against the glass, it looks very appetizing and very impressive, too. If you want to spice things up at your party buffet with some "cool" beverages, you should definitely cast this one.

Serving size: 1

Prep Time: 10 mins

Ingredients:

- ¼ cup fresh cucumber juice
- 1 tbsp fresh lemon juice
- 1 tbsp fresh lime juice
- 1 tbsp agave syrup
- 1 pc European cucumber, thinly sliced
- ¼ tsp dill, finely chopped
- 1 tbsp water
- ¼ cup chilled club soda
- ¼ cup ice cubes

Instructions:

1. Arrange the thin cucumber slice into the inside of a glass.

2. Pour in ice.

3. Meanwhile, stir together cucumber, lemon and lime juices, agave syrup, and chopped dill in a cocktail shaker.

4. Pour onto prepared serving glass, top with club soda and a fresh sprig of dill.

5. Serve and enjoy.

Banana Punch

Make your parties delightful with this witty mix of refreshing ingredients. It's crisp and fresh, more appetizing than a regular juice, and would certainly brighten up the beverage spread. This is perfect for pairing with different types of food and can well brighten up your brunch. So, mix up and serve. You will not need so much time to make a good batch for a crowd.

Serving size: 20

Prep Time: 10 mins

Ingredients:

- 2 pcs ripe bananas
- 1 pc orange, sliced
- 4oz frozen orange juice concentrate, thawed
- ¼ cup lemonade concentrate, thawed
- 16oz pineapple juice, chilled
- 2L lemon-lime soda, chilled
- ¾ cups sugar, divided
- 1 cup warm water, divided

Instructions:

1. Blend together bananas, lemonade, and orange juice.

2. Add warm water and half of the sugar into the blender and pulse until smooth. Transfer mixture to a pitcher or a large jug and let it freeze.

3. An hour before you are ready to serve, take out the frozen banana mix.

4. Stir together pineapple juice and lemon-lime soda in a punch bowl, plus the banana mix.

5. Top with orange slices and serve.

Orange Julius Mocktail

Orange Julius is another yummy drink that rightfully deserves a spot in this mocktail recipe book. And if it is not festive enough, we also added eggnog into the mix, so you can easily prepare them for an upcoming special dinner and amaze everyone.

Serving size: 6

Prep Time: 5 mins

Ingredients:

- 1 (6oz) can frozen orange juice concentrate, thawed
- 1 cup eggnog
- 1 tsp vanilla
- ¼ tsp ground nutmeg
- 1/3 cup sugar
- 1 cup water
- 2 cups ice cubes
- Whipped cream

Instructions:

1. Place all the ingredients in a blender, except for the whipped cream, and pulse on high until combined.

2. Pour mixture into serving glasses, add a whipped cream topping and a dash of nutmeg, and you are ready to serve.

Peach Bellini Mocktail

Here is another Bellini mocktail but this time, we are closer to the original recipe, as we are using peaches. It's a refreshing drink that's booze-free and definitely kid-friendly. It's one of the many things you would love to have during hot summer days. And since it is so easy to prepare, you can easily let everyone have an indulgence if they want to.

Serving size: 2

Prep Time: 5 mins

Ingredients:

- 2 pcs ripe peaches, peeled, sliced, and frozen for an hour
- 1 cup sparkling apple juice
- 1 tsp lime juice
- 2 tbsp sugar

Instructions:

1. Place all the ingredients in a blender and pulse until smooth.

2. Transfer into serving glasses. You may add more sparkling juice poured on top if you like it fizzier.

Booze-Free French 75

French 75 is another classic drink made of highly intoxicating ingredients like gin. But with this mocktail, you will have no problem about getting tipsy because it could be the last thing that could happen to you. To give the beverage a twist, we added sparkling water instead of champagne and lemon juice instead of gin. That makes this recipe a good one to share with everyone.

Serving size: 2

Prep Time: 2 mins

Ingredients:

- 2 (8oz) bottles tonic water
- 3oz fresh lemon juice
- 2 pcs rock candy sticks
- ¼ tsp lemon zest
- 2 cups ice

Instructions:

1. Place lemon juice and ice in a cocktail shaker together with some lemon zest.

2. Shake vigorously until frosty, then divide among serving glasses.

3. Gently pour in tonic water and garnish with candy sticks.

4. Serve immediately.

Butterbeer

Just like the Harry Potter series, butterbeer seems like magic! It says 'beer,' but it is in no way alcoholic and is actually delicious enough to serve to your guests, young and old. It's quite fancy and looks very appetizing. The original version has very minimal alcohol content that even underage kids are allowed to drink it but since we are doing a mocktail recipe book, we will drop any of that so even elves can enjoy their butterbeer without worrying about getting drunk.

Serving size: 10

Prep Time: 5 mins

Ingredients:

- 2 L vanilla cream soda
- 2 tbsp butter extract
- 3 tsp rum extract, divided
- 7oz marshmallow creme
- 1 cup whipping cream

Instructions:

1. Stir together cream soda, butter extract, and about 2 teaspoons of rum extract. Let it chill in the fridge while you prepare the topping.

2. For the cream topping, simply mix the whipping and marshmallow cream together with the remaining rum extract on high.

3. To serve, simply pour butterbeer into individual serving glasses, spoon over cream topping, and enjoy.

Conclusion

Just because you can't serve alcohol doesn't mean you have to settle into something boring. You can easily make your beverage menu interesting enough by adding a few mocktail tricks.

Mocktails are fun and crazy even though they are non-alcoholic. Through these wonderful drinks, you can enjoy sangrias, margaritas, mules, daiquiris, and others, minus getting tipsy. You only get the delicious flavors but not the alcohol, that's why. Mocktails are perfect for your parties, where both adults and kids alike can enjoy creative drinks. They can even make a great idea for an afternoon snack or simply as something refreshing to cool you off during the hot days of summer. They are that 'cool' and tasty and versatile.

This mocktails recipe cookbook is for everyone who wants to keep a handful of options in their pantries so they can come up with something explosive when need be. Got some family friends coming over for a barbecue? Going for a picnic? These mocktail recipes are great for those and more!

Happy cooking!

About the Author

Molly Mills always knew she wanted to feed people delicious food for a living. Being the oldest child with three younger brothers, Molly learned to prepare meals at an early age to help out her busy parents. She just seemed to know what spice went with which meat and how to make sauces that would dress up the blandest of pastas. Her creativity in the kitchen was a blessing to a family where money was tight and making new meals every day was a challenge.

Molly was also a gifted athlete as well as chef and secured a Lacrosse scholarship to Syracuse University. This was a blessing to her family as she was the first to go to college and at little cost to her parents. She took full advantage of her college education and earned a business degree. When she graduated, she joined her culinary skills and business acumen into a successful catering business. She wrote her first e-book after a customer asked if she could pay for several of her recipes. This sparked the entrepreneurial spirit in Mills and she thought if one person wanted them, then why not share the recipes with the world!

Molly lives near her family's home with her husband and three children and still cooks for her family every chance she gets. She plays Lacrosse with a local team made up of her old teammates from college and there are always some tasty nibbles on the ready after each game.

Don't Miss Out!

Scan the QR-Code below and you can sign up to receive emails whenever Molly Mills publishes a new book. There's no charge and no obligation.

Sign Me Up

https://molly.gr8.com

Printed in Great Britain
by Amazon